Sisters against Slavery

Sisters against Slavery

A Story about Sarah and
Angelina Grimké

by Stephanie Sammartino
McPherson
illustrated by Karen Ritz

A Creative Minds Biography

Carolrhoda Books, Inc./Minneapolis

To Jennifer, Marianne, Joseph, and Jonathan

The author would like to thank Angelo Sammartino, Richard McPherson, and her editor, Gwenyth Swain, for their help and support.

Text copyright © 1999 by Stephanie Sammartino McPherson
Illustrations copyright © 1999 by Karen Ritz

Carolrhoda Books, Inc.
A Division of the Lerner Publishing Group
241 First Avenue North
Minneapolis, MN 55401 U.S.A.

Website address: www.lernerbooks.com

Library of Congress Cataloging-in-Publication Data

McPherson, Stephanie Sammartino.
   Sisters against slavery : a story about Sarah and Angelina Grimké / by Stephanie Sammartino McPherson ; illustrated by Karen Ritz.
       p.   cm. — (A Creative minds biography)
   Includes bibliographical references and index.
   Summary: A biography of two sisters from a wealthy southern family who devoted their lives to the causes of abolition and women's rights.
   ISBN 1-57505-361-6
   1. Grimké, Angelina Emily, 1805–1879—Juvenile literature. 2. Grimké, Sarah Moore, 1792–1873—Juvenile literature. 3. Women abolitionists—South Carolina—Biography—Juvenile literature. 4. Antislavery movements—United States—History—19th century—Juvenile literature. 5. Feminists—South Carolina—Biography—Juvenile literature. 6. Women's rights—United States—History—19th century—Juvenile literature. 7. Sisters—South Carolina—Biography—Juvenile literature. [1. Grimké, Sarah Moore, 1792–1873.
2. Grimké, Angelina Emily, 1805–1879. 3. Feminists. 4. Abolitionists.
5. Women—Biography.] I. Ritz, Karen, ill. II. Title. III. Series.
E449.G865M46   1999
326'.8'0922—dc21
[B]   98-46741

Manufactured in the United States of America
1 2 3 4 5 6 – MA – 04 03 02 01 00 99

Table of Contents

1

Determined Young Girl

Five-year-old Sarah Grimké was running away from home. Somehow she slipped out of her big, busy house when no one was looking. Tears slid down her cheeks as she wandered along the wharf of Charleston, South Carolina.

Mysterious piles of cargo lined the docks. Sailors swaggered by and called in strange languages. Sarah felt small and alone. Tilting back her head, she stared at the masts of the great ships towering above her. Sarah hoped that one of those ships would take her far away. Who in the noisy confusion of the wharf would help her?

Finally Sarah found a sea captain who listened to her plan. She explained that she didn't care where she went as long as there was no slavery. That morning she had seen a slave whipped. Sarah was terrified. She never wanted to see such cruelty again.

Before the captain could decide what to do, Sarah's anxious nursemaid caught up with her. Soon the little girl was on her way home again, dragged along the docks by the trusted black nurse she called "Mauma." That evening other black servants cooked her dinner and waited on her parents and brothers and sisters. There was no way Sarah could pretend that slavery didn't exist. In the late 1700s, slavery was a way of life in the South.

Born November 26, 1792, Sarah was the sixth of John and Mary Grimké's fourteen children. Her father, a well-respected judge and planter, had fought as a lieutenant colonel in the Revolutionary War years earlier. Her mother managed two homes and watched over an ever-growing family. Sarah was a kind-hearted little girl, anxious to please her parents. But she had strong ideas of her own that sometimes surprised Judge and Mrs. Grimké. Other children didn't question things so eagerly. What made Sarah different?

Sometimes Sarah played with her older sister Mary and younger sister Anna. But her brother Thomas, six years older, became her best friend. As she grew up, Sarah wanted to learn everything Thomas did. The history, science, and geography she studied with her brother were far more exciting than the needlework, music, and drawing she learned with her sisters. The girls also did reading, writing, and simple arithmetic, but there was nothing at school to challenge a bright girl like Sarah.

One day Thomas got a new book filled with words Sarah couldn't understand. Immediately she decided that she wanted to learn Latin with her brother. But to her disappointment, Judge Grimké said no. Her mother agreed that it was silly for a girl to study Latin. Worst of all, Thomas made fun of her ambition. Sarah couldn't understand it. She loved learning and felt she could never get enough new ideas. Her family seemed to think that too many ideas weren't proper for a girl.

Sarah believed that everyone deserved a good education—no matter who they were or what the color of their skin was. Every Sunday after attending St. Philip's Church in Charleston, Sarah, Anna, and Mary read Bible stories to children in the "colored school." Sarah wanted the children to read the Bible for themselves, but teaching a slave to read or write was against state law.

Usually Sarah was an obedient child. But the unfairness of the law boiled up inside her. She had to do something! So Sarah worked out a plan with her personal maid, a slave girl named Hetty who was about her age. At night Sarah blew out the candle in her room and covered the keyhole so no one could see in.

Then she got out her spelling book and sprawled before the fire with Hetty. Sarah slowly taught Hetty to recognize letters, then to put them together to form sounds and words.

Perhaps it was Sarah's mother or one of her sisters or maybe nurse "Mauma" who opened the door one night and discovered what the girls were doing. When the news got back to Judge Grimké, Sarah found herself in big trouble. Her father said she had committed a serious crime and considered having her maidservant whipped. Sarah felt awful. She still hated to see any slave punished. Sometimes she hid in her room crying when she knew one was to be whipped. Luckily, Judge Grimké decided to give the girls a second chance. But they were forbidden to read together.

Sarah could scarcely imagine a life without books. Why should her servant be denied books simply because of her skin color? Such questions became even more troublesome when her family stayed in the country. At the family's Beaufort plantation, Sarah went months without seeing a white person outside her family. She liked the outdoor games and activities of the country, but she hated knowing that the house servants and field-workers weren't free. That's why she loved to get away from it all on horseback.

Cantering through the fields on her lively horse, Hiram, Sarah could forget about slavery for a while.

Sarah's parents didn't understand why she cared so much about their black servants. When Hetty died after a brief illness, Sarah cried and cried. Her parents promised to get her another maid, but Sarah wouldn't hear of it. No one could take the place of her playmate and friend.

In spite of her large family, Sarah was sometimes lonely. She was twelve years old when Thomas left home to go to college. Thomas appreciated his sister's feelings and intelligence in a way that made Sarah feel special. She missed her favorite brother terribly. But when her mother gave birth to another child several months later, Sarah knew that someone else very important had come into her life.

Angelina Emily was born on February 20, 1805. Gazing happily at her tiny sister, Sarah had a wonderful idea. Maybe she could be Angelina's godmother. At first her parents said she was too young, but this was one time Sarah wouldn't take no for an answer. She knew that a godmother was supposed to love, protect, and guide a child. That was exactly what Sarah wanted to do for her much younger sister.

Sarah's determination impressed her parents. At last they agreed that she could be Angelina's godmother.

Sarah held her baby sister during the baptism ceremony at St. Philip's Church and promised to take good care of Angelina.

Sarah kept her promise. In fact, she spent so much time with Angelina that when the little girl began to talk, she called Sarah "Mother." Sarah called the beautiful toddler with the dark curls and large blue eyes "Nina." Even as a small child, Nina expected to get her way. Sarah must have been amused—and sometimes annoyed—by her little sister. Still, she listened carefully to Nina's chatter.

Anyone who saw the girls together might have guessed that Sarah was dreaming of her own child someday. But Sarah's hopes were leaning in a different direction. Secretly she had begun to read her father's law books. Even though it was unheard of for a woman, Sarah Grimké was determined to become a lawyer.

A Small, Powerful Voice

When Thomas returned home after graduation, he was full of exciting ideas. Fifteen-year-old Sarah listened eagerly to everything—especially his views on education. In the early 1800s, many children didn't have the chance to go to school. Thomas believed that education should be available to white boys—and even some talented white girls—everywhere. That was good news to Sarah! And maybe her brother's new plans were good news. Instead of becoming a lawyer as their father wished, Thomas wanted to be a minister. If Thomas managed to change their father's mind, maybe Sarah could, too. Judge Grimké often remarked that Sarah would make a fine lawyer if only she were a boy. She desperately wanted to show him that a girl could also make a fine lawyer.

But Sarah and Thomas were both disappointed. Although Judge Grimké forced his son to become a lawyer, he refused to let his daughter be one. Since Sarah couldn't follow her own path, she did what her parents wanted. She set aside law books and entered Charleston's lively social life. A plain girl with winning manners and a ready smile, Sarah made many friends. She liked to talk and laugh and paint and read. If she still thought about the law, she gave no sign to the fashionable young people she met at balls and parties. But sometimes when she returned home, Sarah felt she had wasted her time. Surely there was more to life than fancy teas and dances. For a while, she gave up parties, turning to charity work and prayer meetings instead. But the invitations kept coming, and soon Sarah was going to parties again. She called this "backsliding" and tried to become more serious.

It was hard to be serious around playful Nina, however. With her youngest sister, Sarah could laugh and forget her conflicts. But Nina had a thoughtful side, too. In some ways, Nina was a lot like her older sister. She had a strong sense of justice and was horrified by the way slaves were treated. One day, when Nina was about eight years old, she was walking by the workhouse, or prison, on her way to a friend's house.

Suddenly she heard a scream of agony. Frightened, she hurried past as more screams rang through the air. Later her friend explained that slaves often cried out when they were punished in the workhouse. Nina hated to walk past the workhouse after that.

But slaves were also punished right in her own household. One night, when the rest of the family was sleeping, Nina crept from her bed and slipped outside with a bottle of oil. She groped through the dark to the slave quarters and rubbed the soothing oil on the back of a servant who had been recently beaten. As the baby of the family, Nina often got away with things. But if her parents had caught her helping slaves, they would have been furious. Still, Nina felt she had to think for herself—even when her parents didn't understand.

In 1818 Judge Grimké became seriously ill. Although Nina's routine didn't change much, Sarah gave up her social life to take care of her father. Despite her nursing, Judge Grimké continued to worsen. Finally local doctors recommended a visit to a specialist in Philadelphia. The judge chose twenty-five-year-old Sarah to accompany him.

For two months, Sarah followed the doctor's instructions and nursed her father in the busy, northern city. Then the doctor suggested a trip to the seashore.

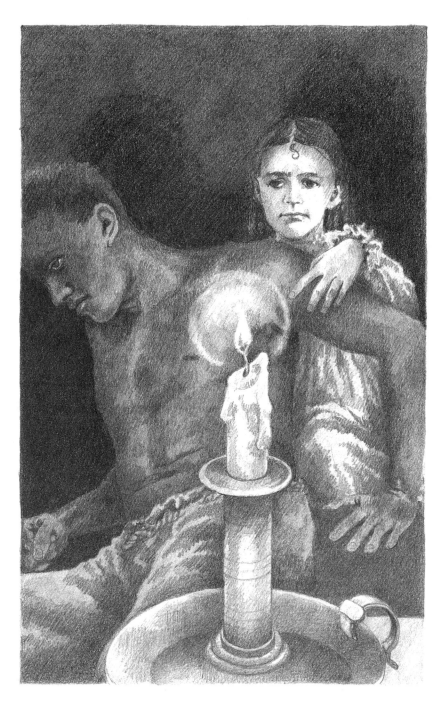

He hoped the fresh air and salt water would help the patient. Sarah took her father by carriage to the remote fishing village of Long Branch, New Jersey. But Judge Grimké was never well enough to leave his room. Sarah was all alone with her father when he died on August 8, 1819.

After a simple funeral, Sarah took the carriage back to Philadelphia. She stayed with a Quaker family there while she mourned her father and thought about her life. When she finally returned to Charleston, she met more Quakers on the boat. Curious as always, Sarah listened to Israel Morris, a respected merchant and father of eight, discuss his religious beliefs. By the time the boat reached Charleston, Sarah had learned a great deal about the Society of Friends, or Quakers.

Nursing her father had given Sarah inner strength and courage. Yet, in some ways, she felt almost as alone at home as she had in Philadelphia. Her brothers and sisters had their own lives. Sarah grew discouraged and so nervous she hardly knew what to do. Even fourteen-year-old Nina, popular and outgoing, wasn't sure what to make of her suddenly strange "Mother."

During this time, Sarah read a book on the Society of Friends that Israel had given her. One day, instead of going to church services with her family, she went alone to the small Quaker Meetinghouse. Slipping quietly onto a plain, wooden bench, Sarah stuck out as a visitor. But she also felt at home. She found the simplicity of the Friends Meeting deeply moving.

Sarah knew it would be very difficult to become a Quaker in her hometown. Her friends and neighbors wouldn't understand. But Sarah believed that God was calling her to be a Quaker. A small but powerful voice deep inside her also said that God wanted her to move North. This was a shocking message. In the 1820s, unmarried women didn't leave their families. Even though Sarah felt she had "an unmistakable call, not to be disregarded," she was a little worried. She begged her widowed sister Anna Frost to come with her. Anna agreed, and on May 15, 1821, the sisters and Anna's young daughter boarded a ship for Philadelphia.

Angelina Takes Sides

Israel Morris, whose wife had died the previous year, welcomed Sarah to the city. He invited her to stay in his home called Greenhill Farm. Since Anna found her own lodgings, Sarah didn't see her sister every day. Her Quaker friends became her second family. Sarah lived a quiet life and attended meetings of the Society of Friends every week. She got to know Israel's eight children, helped with household duties, and discussed religion. In keeping with Friends' rules, she didn't wear bright colors, but she liked pretty clothes. Some of her dresses were stylishly cut. One day while she was getting dressed, Sarah decided it was time to give up fashion completely. After that, the lines of her dresses were as plain as the colors.

When Sarah took a trip to South Carolina, her somber clothes startled her family. But back in Philadelphia, Sarah looked right at home among the simply dressed Friends. She moved in with Israel's sister, Catherine Morris, and did charity work. After she joined the Society of Friends, she also thought about becoming a minister. Although other churches didn't allow women preachers, Quakers let women speak at their weekly meetings. But whenever Sarah rose to speak at meeting, she grew shy before so many people. She stumbled over her words or rushed through them too quickly. Several Quakers privately pointed out that she was hard to understand. Sarah wondered if she would ever make a good minister, but she kept trying.

Israel Morris may have understood her struggles. Sarah enjoyed spending time with Israel. She wasn't too surprised when he asked her to be his wife on September 16, 1826. Sarah looked at the handsome, middle-aged widower and knew that she loved him enough to marry him. But she also knew that she couldn't say yes. Perhaps Sarah felt she had to give her whole life to religion, or perhaps she felt over-whelmed by the thought of caring for eight children. As kindly as possible, Sarah turned down Israel's pro-posal. The two promised to remain friends.

Sarah still missed her family in Charleston. In November 1827, six years after moving North, she set sail for another visit home.

More than anyone else in the family, Angelina wanted to understand Sarah and to know more of her views. Although only twenty-two, Angelina was more outgoing and sure of herself than her thirty-four-year-old sister was. Where Sarah was cautious and conventional, Angelina was eager, headstrong, and used to getting her way. Angelina was also very curious. As she learned more from her older sister, Angelina slowly began to find new meaning in the Quaker clothing that had seemed so dreary on Sarah's last visit. She began to think she should give up pleasures for her own spiritual good. On January 10, 1828, Angelina started a new diary. "Today I have torn up my Novels," she wrote.

That was just the beginning of Angelina's sacrifices. She went through her closet, snatching at veils and lengths of lace. Soon a heap of elegance lay on her bed. Angelina enjoyed her fancy clothes, but she knew she didn't need them. With her usual determination, she carried them straight to Sarah, who stuffed them into a cushion. Later, Angelina even began to copy Quaker speech patterns, using "thee" and "thou" instead of "you."

The next summer, Angelina went to visit Sarah, who had returned to Philadelphia. For the first time in her life, Angelina was surrounded by Quakers. She visited many of their homes with Sarah and always felt welcome. But as a Southerner, she couldn't escape questions about slavery. Sometimes Angelina had to blink back tears as her host or hostess pressed her for her views. Although she believed slaves should be treated kindly, she hadn't condemned slavery in the same way Sarah had. Her mother and brothers and friends in Charleston all owned slaves. Angelina didn't know what to say when people told her that slavery itself was a terrible evil even if the slaves were treated well. In the end, however, she had to admit the Quakers were right. No matter how you looked at it, slavery was wrong.

When Angelina returned to Charleston in November, she was determined to convince her family and friends to give up slavery. The problem was they refused to be convinced. Dressed in her plain Quaker garb, as sure of herself as ever, Angelina quarreled with almost everyone. "Would'st thou be willing to be a slave thyself?" she asked over and over. Of course not, her neighbors replied, but they either refused to agree that slavery was wrong or believed that nothing could be done about it.

Angelina argued passionately until her friends began to desert her. Even her brother Henry turned on her when she criticized him for punishing his slaves. He told her she "had come from the North expressly to be miserable . . . and make everyone in the house so."

Finally Angelina realized that Charleston was no longer her home. In November 1829, she set sail for Philadelphia again, this time for good. Angelina was twenty-four years old, fired with conviction, and eager to begin a new life with her sister. She enjoyed shopping for food in the open-air market and doing chores that slaves had done for her before. Every week she attended meetings of the Society of Friends, and she became a member in 1831.

After Angelina was officially a Friend, a young man named Edward Bettle began to visit her. Angelina welcomed his attention, but she hoped for a career as well as marriage. That's one reason she was thrilled when Catharine Beecher, a pioneer educator, came to Philadelphia. Angelina couldn't hear enough about the school the famous teacher had opened for women in Connecticut.

Without asking permission from the Society of Friends, Angelina traveled to see Catharine Beecher's school for herself. Soon Angelina was so excited by the school that she had little time to worry about what her Quaker friends thought. Catharine Beecher believed women deserved a solid education as much as men and that they should use their knowledge for the good of society.

When Angelina returned to Philadelphia, she was determined to attend Catharine Beecher's school and become a teacher. But she hadn't known how many people she would upset. Quaker friends said that she shouldn't go live with those who didn't share her religion. Even Sarah urged her to reconsider. Worst of all, Edward Bettle stopped calling on her. Angelina was deeply hurt. Finally she told the Friends that she had made a mistake and would not attend the school after all.

Angelina took up her old life and tried to be happy. She studied, read the Bible, taught at a Quaker school for small children, and wondered when Edward Bettle would come to see her again. Months passed before Edward suddenly reappeared. He still loved Angelina, and she felt a rush of tenderness for her old suitor.

Before Edward could ask Angelina to marry him, however, he died of cholera in the fall of 1832. Numb with grief, Angelina was further shattered when Edward's parents told her not to come to the funeral. They felt she had wavered in her loyalty and caused their son pain. In her sorrow, Angelina turned to Sarah for comfort and support.

In many ways, the two sisters were still outsiders in the Society of Friends. Sarah had been discouraged in her hope to be a minister. Angelina was much too independent to be bound by Friends' rules. Although Quakers disapproved of slavery, orthodox (traditional) Friends didn't meddle in worldly affairs. They felt it was enough not to own slaves themselves. Slavery, they believed, would end as more people realized how wrong it was to own another human being. Angelina was terribly impatient with the orthodox Quaker approach. When she believed strongly in a cause, she wanted to *do* something about it.

Some people, called abolitionists, were already banding together to fight slavery. Although Angelina knew that orthodox Friends frowned on abolitionist activities, she began reading antislavery newspapers early in 1834. She just had to know what was happening in the movement to abolish slavery. For years, people had talked about freeing the slaves slowly over a period of time. But lately, some abolitionists had demanded freedom NOW.

In her heart, Angelina applauded their arguments. She joined the Philadelphia Female Anti-Slavery Society and served on a committee to help people of color improve their lives. Angelina's Quaker friends were shocked. To Angelina, this must have seemed very strange. The same people who persuaded her to renounce slavery in the first place didn't want her to fight to end it.

Meanwhile more people were coming to fear and hate the abolitionists. In Charleston, a load of antislavery literature was burned at the post office. Angelina was so upset by the events that for a while she almost stopped reading. Then the *Liberator,* an important antislavery newspaper, arrived, and she had to know what it said. Her eyes filled with tears as she read the stirring words of William Lloyd Garrison. The noted abolitionist and publisher had recently been attacked and dragged through the streets of Boston with a rope around his neck. He begged people to reject violence and let the antislavery speakers be heard.

For several days, Angelina thought about the article and all the recent hostility. Then she sat down to write to William Lloyd Garrison. She agreed with him that ending slavery was more important than any danger. In fact, she almost welcomed the hardship the abolitionists faced. "I feel as if I could say, LET IT COME;" she wrote, "for it is my deep, solemn, deliberate conviction, that *this is a cause worth dying for.*"

29

Sarah Joins the Fight

Several weeks after Angelina wrote her letter, she received an unexpected visitor. Samuel Bettle had had little to do with Angelina since the death of his son. Yet he stood in the drawing room glowering as he thrust a newspaper into her hands. Angelina stared at the paper and stifled a gasp. There was her letter, exactly as she had written it to William Lloyd Garrison. Although she'd suspected her letter might be published, she'd never imagined the famous abolitionist would print her name.

Samuel Bettle was furious. He told Angelina she had disgraced the name of Grimké, and he asked her to take back publicly what she had written to Garrison. Angelina refused Bettle's request. She stuck by her letter and continued to attend antislavery meetings.

There she made several black friends. The stories these new friends shared shocked both Sarah and Angelina. Even in the North, even in the Society of Friends, racial prejudice existed. Apart from the slavery question, it seemed that many white people didn't want to mix with black people socially. The sisters had never paid much attention to the "colored bench" in their Meetinghouse. As they learned more, the bench began to disturb them greatly.

In February 1836, Sarah and Angelina traveled to Providence, Rhode Island, for a large, regional gathering of the Society of Friends. Suddenly their whole world opened up. Not all Quakers were as rigid as members of their own meeting were. To their delight, they met many Friends who were strong abolitionists. In their company, the sisters felt relaxed and free to speak openly.

After the meeting, Sarah and Angelina couldn't bear to return to Philadelphia. Their old life seemed almost like a prison.

That summer Sarah went to Burlington, Vermont, while Angelina visited friends in Shrewsbury, New Jersey. The two sisters wrote long letters to one another as they worked out their feelings. Once Sarah had guided Angelina. Now it was Angelina's turn to lead the way.

Although Sarah condemned slavery with all her heart, she still wasn't sure it was up to her to change things. Angelina urged Sarah to go one step farther and work to end slavery.

But Angelina wasn't sure how to do this herself. Impatient to act, she asked over and over what she could do to help. Finally, after a sleepless night, she arrived at breakfast with a determined look in her eye. "It has all come to me," she announced. "I can write an appeal to Southern women."

Mrs. Parker, Angelina's Quaker hostess, stared in surprise. Abolitionists faced enough resentment in the North. Their arguments were sure to stir up anger in the South. In any case, what could women do? Before her hostess could protest, Angelina continued, "I will speak to them in such tones that they *must* hear me." As a Southerner herself, Angelina believed she could touch other Southerners—and especially Southern women—in a way that Northern abolitionists could not.

For the next several days, words seemed to pour out of Angelina. Then in the middle of her task, a letter arrived that threw her into turmoil. It was from Elizur Wright, the secretary of the American Anti-Slavery Society. He wanted Angelina to come to New York to speak against slavery.

Here was an opportunity that went beyond anything Angelina had ever imagined. In the middle 1800s, American women almost never spoke in public. Their whole lives were supposed to center around the home and family.

Even though Wright suggested that she talk in private homes to women only, Angelina trembled at the thought of what he suggested. She knew how bold, even shocking, her conduct would appear. And why had Wright singled her out in the first place? To her surprise, Angelina discovered that the letter she'd written to Garrison had been widely reprinted in other reform newspapers and church magazines. Tens of thousands of copies had been printed as a pamphlet and sent all over the North. Already Angelina had a reputation!

Angelina wasn't ready to accept Wright's proposal. Instead she told him about her writing project and promised to send it to him when she was done. "I know you do not make the laws," she wrote in her

Appeal to the Christian Women of the South, "but I also know that *you are the wives and mothers, the sisters and daughters of those who do;* and if you really suppose *you* can do nothing to overthrow slavery, you are greatly mistaken." Angelina urged women to free their slaves and to pay them wages if their former slaves wished to remain as servants. The women should also help freed slaves become educated.

As soon as she was done, Angelina rushed her manuscript off to New York and told Elizur Wright to print her name with it. Within weeks, the appeal was published. Once more, Angelina's Quaker friends blamed her for getting involved in a worldly cause and drawing attention to herself.

People in her hometown were furious, too. When copies of the appeal arrived in Charleston, the postmasters publicly burned them. The mayor told Mrs. Grimké that Angelina would be arrested if she returned to South Carolina. Friends in Charleston wrote to Angelina that she might even be attacked by a mob. Angelina hadn't seen her mother in six years. It hurt to know that she couldn't go home.

But facing opposition made Angelina strong. She accepted Elizur Wright's invitation to become a speaker for the American Anti-Slavery Society. Sarah was quick to point out the difficulties, but Angelina had made up her mind. "I *must* go," she declared. Sarah had to decide what she would do. Should she listen to her Quaker friends or should she join her sister? Then, to her surprise, Sarah received a letter from her mother begging her to go with Angelina. Although Mrs. Grimké didn't approve of her daughter's plan, she didn't want Angelina to be alone.

Her mother's letter gave Sarah the push she needed. In November of 1836, she accompanied Angelina to a special convention in New York that would train new speakers for the antislavery society. Soon Sarah forgot her worries. At last she had found a place that both welcomed and challenged her! Not long before, Sarah had disapproved of Angelina's writing. But she was so inspired by the convention that she began to write, too. Ideas, she discovered, flowed more easily when she wasn't facing an audience. In her *Epistle to the Clergy of the Southern States,* she urged ministers to speak out against slavery.

At the convention, the sisters met William Lloyd Garrison, a surprisingly gentle and quiet man. Could this be the fearless publisher who was so hated and scorned outside abolitionist groups? They saw Theodore Weld, another great abolitionist who was sometimes called "the most mobbed man in the United States."

Like Garrison, Weld wasn't at all what Sarah and Angelina expected. Watching him walk onto the stage, Angelina thought he looked so ordinary. Then he began to talk, and Angelina saw him transformed into a powerful and brilliant crusader. He seemed to speak directly to her as he described the rights and dignity of all human beings.

By the time the training convention ended, word of the new female antislavery speakers had spread. So many women wanted to hear the sisters speak that the biggest parlor couldn't hold them all. Finally a Baptist minister offered them a room in his church. This promised to be a more public event than either Sarah or Angelina had imagined. Other abolitionists also worried about the arrangements. They feared the spectacle of women speaking in public would "do more harm than good" to the antislavery cause.

Just before the scheduled meeting, Theodore Weld came to visit Sarah and Angelina at their lodgings. He told them they were doing the right thing and not to be afraid. Heartened by his support, the sisters went to the church. About three hundred women were waiting for them.

Angelina spoke first. With deep feeling, she described her firsthand knowledge of slavery. Then Sarah stood up. If it was hard to stand up at Friends

Meeting, this was even worse. But Sarah had steeled herself for this moment. Forgetting her own worries, she thought only of the people she was trying to help. The audience responded warmly.

Over the next two months, so many people wanted to hear Sarah and Angelina that they had to move their lectures into the church itself. They climbed the steps to the pulpit so that everyone could see and hear them. Of course, this shocked their opponents more than ever. But Theodore Weld was delighted with their success.

During their time in New York, the sisters often joined Theodore when he visited the sick or needy. Angelina admired the way he put the welfare of others above his own. She loved the way his face lit up when he spoke. Although both sisters respected and liked Theodore, Angelina was beginning to feel something deeper.

But everyone knew that Theodore had vowed not to marry until slavery ended. And if Angelina hoped to change his mind, she was soon disappointed. When the sisters were ready to return to Philadelphia, Theodore seemed unconcerned—even distant. Once again, Angelina's romantic dreams were crushed.

Women Must Do It

Sarah and Angelina weren't giving a speech, but they knew they would cause a stir as they entered the room. They also knew they had no choice. They were back at their old Friends Meetinghouse where the colored bench still cruelly divided the worshipers. Before anyone could stop them, the sisters squeezed into the pew and sat down with their black friends. The white Quakers could stare as much as they wanted. Never again would Sarah and Angelina Grimké accept racial discrimination.

In May when the sisters returned to New York City, they continued to fight prejudice—this time through their writing. In outrage, Angelina wrote, "[White Americans] refuse to eat, or ride, or walk, or associate [with]. . . people of color, unless they visit them in the capacity of *servants.* . . . Who ever heard of a more wicked absurdity?"

Soon the American Anti-Slavery Society sent the sisters to New England for another speaking tour. Boston seemed more tolerant and open-minded than any other place they'd visited. Full of hope, Sarah and Angelina set out for their first talk on June 6, 1837. The small town of Quincy, Massachusetts, lay on the sisters' route to their appointment in Dorchester. Although Sarah and Angelina were pressed for time, they stopped to speak with John Quincy Adams, then a representative to Congress from Massachusetts. When Angelina asked if he believed women could help end slavery, the former president smiled. "If it is abolished, *they* must do it," he said.

Thinking of his words must certainly have inspired Sarah and Angelina when they arrived at their meeting. More than a hundred women were spilling out of the parlor in the private house where they were scheduled to speak. The sisters and their eager audience had to hustle to the town hall so everyone could hear them.

From town to town, the Grimké sisters traveled, bumping along dirt roads in stagecoaches and open wagons. They slept in the homes of sympathetic listeners and sometimes went hungry because they refused to eat foods that slaves might have grown in the South. Although they were often tired and sick, they spoke almost every day. But none of these hardships mattered when Sarah and Angelina stood before an audience in a rural church or town hall.

Almost from the beginning, small numbers of men crept into their lectures. Sarah and Angelina didn't mind. The more people who heard their speeches, the better. Then in Amesbury, Massachusetts, two men challenged the sisters. The men had recently visited the South and felt slaves weren't much worse off than Northern factory workers. Angelina agreed to debate them.

Crowds of people turned out for two evenings of debate. Electrifying the audience, Angelina told of slaves whose children had been sold and marriages broken up. She spoke of separated families who couldn't even send letters because slaves were forbidden to read or write. Angelina looked out at the sea of people. These women and men enjoyed books and newspapers. They kept in touch with loved ones far away. They would do anything to protect their children. Angelina's voice was calm, but her eyes blazed.

Were the workers of Amesbury really as bad off as the slaves? she demanded. No one dared say yes.

Despite the Grimkés' success, many people still thought women shouldn't get involved in important issues like slavery. One of them was Catharine Beecher, the teacher whose school Angelina had visited. Miss Beecher published an essay saying that women shouldn't work for abolitionist societies and shouldn't send petitions to Congress.

With all her heart, Angelina believed in the rightness of what she was doing. She couldn't let Miss Beecher's message go unchallenged, and she couldn't risk losing the help that women could give the abolitionist movement. In a series of newspaper essays called *Letters to Catherine* [sic] *E. Beecher,* Angelina urged all women to become involved in political issues. "I believe it is woman's right to have a voice in all the laws and regulations by which she is to be governed," Angelina declared.

Even more than her sister, Sarah felt driven to champion women's rights. She had been denied the education and legal career she deeply wanted. In spite of that, she was doing and saying things few people would have imagined possible for a woman. Sarah had stopped accepting limits other people set for her. She wanted other women to do the same.

Through writing, Sarah could spread her views to the largest possible audience. In her newspaper series, *Letters on the Equality of the Sexes,* Sarah encouraged women to stand up for their rights.

By this time, many people were more than annoyed by the Grimké sisters' activities. They were also scared. Some opponents charged that Angelina would be better named "Devilina." Finally a group of ministers in Massachusetts were so upset that they wrote a letter to be read in all their churches. They warned of "the dangers which at present seem to threaten the female character with wide spread and permanent injury." The letter didn't mention Sarah and Angelina by name, but everyone knew who the ministers were talking about.

Sarah Grimké took up her pen to reply. She agreed there was a danger all right, but not the one the ministers meant. The danger was from men who tried to keep women from assuming their rightful place in society. "Men and women were CREATED EQUAL;" she wrote, "they are both moral and accountable beings, and whatever is *right* for man to do, is *right* for woman."

Fewer churches were open to the Grimkés after the ministers' letter, but they continued to talk and to write as fearlessly as ever. They spoke in city halls, theaters, even barns. Women trudged up to eight miles through wilderness and rough country roads to hear the sisters speak. Sometimes so many people came that they couldn't all fit in a single hall. Then the sisters had to split up. While Sarah spoke in one place, Angelina spoke in another. In Andover, more than eight hundred people braved a thunderstorm to hear the sisters' message. At Woonsocket Falls, even more people crowded into the church. As Sarah talked, she heard a crack as if wood were splintering. One of the beams holding up the balcony had collapsed. Quickly the meeting ended.

During their six-month tour, the Grimké sisters appeared before more than forty thousand people at eighty-five meetings. Some of the people came to hear Angelina speak against slavery, others to hear Sarah explain her views on women's rights. Angelina spoke so powerfully that one minister wrote, "Never...have I seen an audience so held and so moved by any public speaker, man or woman." Sarah's speaking style wasn't as exciting as her sister's was, but she wrote and said things about women that few people had dared suggest before: Women, Sarah firmly believed, deserved the same quality of education as men. Women should get the same wages for doing the same work as men. Most daring of all, women should have a say in making the laws.

Such strong statements made some abolitionists nervous. The sisters were supposed to be talking about slavery—not women. Maybe what they said was true, but this wasn't the time to say it. These men feared that discussing women's rights took attention away from the suffering of the slaves. Theodore Weld, who often wrote to the sisters, agreed. He told them they should concentrate on abolition and leave "the lesser work to others." Hurt and angry, Angelina wrote back. "Can you not see that woman could do and would do a hundred times more for the slave, if she were not fettered?"

Angelina and Sarah went right on giving speech after speech. By November, Angelina was so exhausted that she had to stop speaking in the middle of a lecture. That night she became ill with fever. A very worried Sarah took Angelina to the home of friends in Brookline, Massachusetts. For the moment, their tour was ended.

6

Violent Ending

Angelina had regained her strength by early the next year when an abolitionist named Henry Stanton came to visit. Half playfully, Stanton suggested that Angelina speak before the Massachusetts state legislature. Angelina smiled and made a joking reply. She couldn't tell if Stanton was serious or not. After all, no American woman had ever spoken before a government body before. But after Stanton left, she thought about it again. The men in the legislature had the power to do a great deal for the antislavery cause. There were so many things Angelina could tell them. Finally she decided she *had* to speak. "I feel that this is the most important step I have ever been called to take," she said.

Then something important happened in Angelina's personal life. Ten days before her speech, she got a letter from Theodore Weld.

"I know it will surprise and even amaze you, Angelina," Theodore wrote, "when I say to you as I now do, that for a long time, *you have had my whole heart...*" Angelina stared in joyful wonder. Her teacher, critic, and dear friend was in love with her! At last Angelina could stop fighting her own feelings and admit that she loved him, too. She longed to see Theodore again but was a little afraid to have him come to the legislative meeting. Between speaking and seeing Theodore, she thought she might be overcome with emotion.

Even though Theodore didn't attend her talk, Angelina was still overwhelmed. As she entered the Massachusetts State House on February 21, 1838, she felt faint. The room was jammed. People were standing in the aisles and the doorways. The gallery and the stairs that led to it were full of spectators.

Angelina trembled slightly as she stood on the speakers' platform. She felt very alone without Sarah, who was suffering from a severe cold. When Angelina began talking, however, she was as passionate and convincing as ever. Movingly she explained why twenty thousand women had signed their names to the antislavery petitions that she had brought to the legislature. By the time she was finished, many of Angelina's listeners were crying.

The next few weeks were busy ones as Sarah and Angelina completed an important series of lectures in Boston's Odeon Theater. When the sisters finally left the city on April 23, 1838, they had doubled the number of abolitionists in New England. A crowd of friends and well-wishers came to wave them off.

Less than one month later on May 14, Angelina and Theodore were married at Anna Frost's home in Philadelphia. About forty guests, including two former slaves, prayed with a black minister, then a white minister. They heard Theodore protest the laws that gave a husband automatic control over everything his wife owned. Then everyone signed the marriage certificate before the couple cut their wedding cake. Angelina had made sure it contained no sugar grown by slaves.

Two days later, the wedding seemed a distant memory as Angelina prepared to speak at a convention in Philadelphia's brand-new Pennsylvania Hall. An unruly mob gathered outside, angered at seeing black and white people enter together. Even when a menacing band of protesters broke into the building, Angelina remained calm. Hisses, boos, and insults came from the doorway as she rose to begin her talk. "As a Southerner I feel that it is my duty to stand up here tonight and bear testimony against slavery."

Angelina continued to speak as stones hit the windows and splinters of glass fell on the floor. "What would the breaking of every window be? What would the levelling of this Hall be?" she demanded. "What if the mob should now burst in upon us, break up our meeting and commit violence upon our persons—would this be anything compared with what the slaves endure?"

Perhaps the people attending the conference remembered her words the next day when an even bigger mob surrounded the building. This time the commotion grew so wild that the abolitionists were forced to leave. Sarah and Angelina linked arms with black women to help protect them as they stepped outdoors. Braving jeers and flying rocks, the women made their way through the crowd. Later that evening, Sarah and Angelina learned that Pennsylvania Hall had been burned to the ground.

7

Lifetimes of Commitment

As if the fire had never happened, Sarah and Angelina got up the next morning and prepared for the convention. Ashes drifted through the air as the antislavery women walked past the rubble of Pennsylvania Hall to meet at a school. Sarah felt that the mob proved that the "spirit of slavery" was alive in the North. The way to stop it was to end all separation between black and white Americans. They should sit together in church and walk together on the street. They should work together and befriend one another. Even for an abolitionist, these were bold views. But for the rest of their lives, Sarah and Angelina worked for racial equality.

After the convention, they moved with Theodore to a house in rural Fort Lee, New Jersey. Angelina was determined to show everyone that a public lecturer could also be a good homemaker. She and Sarah learned to cook and clean. Sometimes Angelina burned her stewed apples, but she made delicious bread.

Sarah and Angelina arranged their household chores to give them plenty of time to continue their real work—fighting slavery. They helped Theodore go through thousands of Southern newspapers for a book he was writing about slavery. For six months, they spent hours a day cutting out news stories about runaway slaves, trials, and cruelty against slaves. They also wrote from their firsthand knowledge. Angelina remembered a slave who had jumped from a second-story window to escape from her master as he beat her. Sarah recalled old, sick slaves left to die alone in cold, miserable shacks. No one who read Theodore's book, *American Slavery As It Is,* could possibly say that slaves were treated fairly.

Although Angelina had hoped to return to public life, soon she was happily caring for her first baby, Charles Stuart, born December 14, 1839. Sarah, badly needed at home, was glad to help. The next year the family moved to a fifty-acre farm in Belleville, New Jersey. Theodore still worked for the antislavery society, but he didn't make much money. Although the sisters had to budget carefully, they invited almost everyone they knew to visit them at the farm. Often they gave their guests cold meals because they only cooked hot food once a week. It saved time for more important things.

In 1841 Angelina gave birth to her second son, Theodore (nicknamed Sody). Three years later her daughter, Sarah, was born. Aunt Sarah was like a second mother to the children. When they grew older, she helped Angelina teach them to read and write at home. To make ends meet, Sarah and Angelina began accepting other students, too. Finally, in 1851, Theodore turned the farm into a boarding school.

By the fall of 1854, the sisters were teaching in a new school. The Welds and Sarah had moved to the Raritan Bay Union, a community where many families lived and worked together. While Theodore ran the school, Angelina, age forty-nine, taught history and took care of the children when they were hurt or sick. At age sixty-two, Sarah taught French and acted as a loving grandmother to the students.

Thin and gray-haired, the sisters did look like typical grandmothers—except that they wore bloomers! The loose-fitting pants under short skirts were practical, but people often laughed at the outfit. At last

Sarah and Angelina got tired of the fuss and returned to long dresses.

When the Civil War broke out in 1861, most women put their rights on hold and concentrated on the war effort. Sarah and Angelina usually opposed war, but they firmly believed in the Northern cause. They applauded the Emancipation Proclamation, which freed slaves in the rebel states, but knew it was not enough. All slaves had to be free. "I feel as a South Carolinian, I am bound to tell the North, go on! go on!" said Angelina. "Never falter, never abandon the principles which you have adopted."

Three years after the war, Sarah, Angelina, and Theodore moved to Hyde Park, Massachusetts. The Weld children were grown by then, but the sisters were still surrounded by young people. They taught school in Boston, and for a year they shared their large home with thirteen girl boarders.

One day Angelina was reading a newspaper article about education for African Americans. A young black man, a former slave, had recently made a speech at a nearby college. Angelina caught her breath. The student's name was Grimkie. Could the spelling be wrong? Thinking the young man might have a connection to her family, she wrote him a letter.

Within days, Angelina received a reply. The correct spelling was Grimké, after all! But Archibald Grimké and his brothers Francis and John were more than former Grimké family slaves. They were her nephews, the sons of Angelina's brother Henry. Their mother was a former slave named Nancy Weston. "Of course you know more about my father than I do," Archibald wrote of Henry Grimké.

Angelina was overcome with emotion. She'd half expected to learn Archibald was related, and she could hardly wait to learn more about him. At a time when many Americans would have ignored black relatives, Sarah and Angelina lovingly welcomed their nephews to the family. Although John remained in the South, Sarah and Angelina enjoyed many visits from Frank and Archie through the years. They helped support them through school. To their joy, Archie became a lawyer while Frank became a minister.

Sarah and Angelina knew that Archie and Frank would work hard to promote equality. As involved with political issues as ever, the sisters rejoiced when a constitutional amendment gave black men the right to vote. But what about women? After the war, women had begun to work for their rights once again. Sarah and Angelina became vice presidents of the Massachusetts Woman Suffrage Association.

On March 7, 1870, accompanied by Theodore, the sisters led a parade of forty-two women and many men through a raging snowstorm. The bitter wind stung their faces and blighted the flowers that each woman held. Breaking the law, seventy-seven-year-old Sarah and sixty-five-year-old Angelina were going to vote.

When the women reached the polling place, they found a hostile crowd waiting to laugh at them. But as Sarah and Angelina stepped into the hall, the people watched in silence. Somehow they couldn't jeer at the dignified, courageous old ladies. Instead the spectators moved back to give them space and clapped loudly as the women voted. The votes were discarded, but Sarah and Angelina deeply believed that someday women's votes would count.

Until they died, Sarah at age eighty-one and Angelina at age seventy-four, each sister continued to work for that day. "We are willing to bear the brunt of the storm, if we can only be the means of making a breach in the wall of public opinion," Angelina once wrote. Thanks to Sarah and Angelina Grimké, the wall began to tumble. In their words and in their lives, they showed that all people, men and women, black and white, are equal.

Bibliography

Bacon, Margaret Hope. *Mothers of Feminism: The Story of Quaker Women in America.* San Francisco: Harper & Row, Publishers, 1986.

Barnes, Gilbert H. and Dumond, Dwight L., editors. *Letters of Theodore Dwight Weld, Angelina Grimké Weld and Sarah Grimké, 1822–1844.* 1934. Reprint, New York: Da Capo, 1970.

Bartlett, Elizabeth Ann, editor. *Letters on the Equality of the Sexes and Other Essays by Sarah Grimké.* New Haven, Conn.: Yale University Press, 1988.

Birney, Catherine H. *Sarah and Angelina Grimké: The First American Women Advocates of Abolition and Woman's Rights.* 1885. Reprint, St. Clair Shores, Mich.: Scholarly Press, 1970.

Ceplair, Larry, editor. *The Public Years of Sarah and Angelina Grimké: Selected Writings, 1835–1839.* New York: Columbia University Press, 1989.

Du Pre Lumpkin, Katherine. *The Emancipation of Angelina Grimké.* Chapel Hill, N.C.: University of North Carolina Press, 1974.

Flexner, Eleanor. *Century of Struggle: The Woman's Rights Movement in the United States.* Revised edition. Cambridge, Mass.: The Belknap Press of Harvard University Press, 1975.

Gurko, Miriam. *The Ladies of Seneca Falls: The Birth of the Woman's Rights Movement.* New York: Macmillan Publishing Co., Inc., 1974.

Lerner, Gerda. *The Grimké Sisters from South Carolina: Pioneers for Woman's Rights and Abolition.* New York: Schocken Books, 1971.

Lutz, Alma. *Crusade for Freedom: Women of the Antislavery Movement.* Boston, Mass.: Beacon, 1968.

Melder, Keith E. *Beginnings of Sisterhood: The American Woman's Rights Movement, 1800–1850.* New York: Schocken Books, 1977.

Miller, William Lee. *Arguing About Slavery: John Quincy Adams and the Great Battle in the United States Congress.* New York: Vintage Books, 1995.

Nies, Judith. *Seven Women: Portraits from the American Radical Tradition.* New York: The Viking Press, 1977.

Willimon, William and Patricia. *Turning the World Upside Down: The Story of Sarah and Angelina Grimké.* Columbia, S.C.: Sandlapper Press, Inc., 1972.

Yellin, Jean Fagan. *Women & Sisters: The Antislavery Feminists in American Culture.* New Haven, Conn.: Yale University Press, 1989.

Index

about slavery, 7, 11, 12, 32, 56; relationship with sister Angelina, 13, 15, 32; as speaker, 37–38, 40–41, 44–46; as teacher, 55, 56; writings, 35, 44

Grimké, Thomas (brother), 8, 9, 12, 14, 15

Hetty (slave to Sarah Grimké), 9, 11, 12

Letters on the Equality of the Sexes, 44

Letters to Catherine [sic] *E. Beecher,* 43

Liberator, 28

Massachusetts state legislature, 47, 48

Massachusetts Woman Suffrage Association, 57

"Mauma" (nursemaid to Sarah Grimké), 8, 11

Morris, Catherine, 21

Morris, Israel, 18, 20, 21

Parker, Mrs., 32

Pennsylvania Hall, 50, 51, 53

Philadelphia Female Anti-Slavery Society, 27

Philadelphia, Penn., 16, 18, 19, 21, 24, 25, 26, 31, 38

Quakers. *See* Society of Friends

Raritan Bay Union, 55

slavery, 7, 8, 24, 27, 28, 32, 33, 37, 40, 41, 43, 45, 46, 50, 53, 54, 56

Society of Friends, 18, 19, 20, 21, 22, 24, 25, 26, 27, 31, 32, 34, 35, 39

Stanton, Henry, 47

Weld, Angelina Grimké. *See* Grimké, Angelina

Weld, Charles Stuart (son of Angelina), 54

Weld, Sarah (daughter of Angelina), 55

Weld, Theodore (husband of Angelina), 35, 37, 38, 46, 47–48, 50, 54–55, 56, 59

Weld, Theodore (son of Angelina), 55

Weston, Nancy, 57

women's rights, 26, 43, 44, 45, 46, 56, 57, 59

Wright, Elizur, 33, 34

About the Author

Stephanie Sammartino McPherson enjoys telling the stories of courageous figures overlooked in history books. While researching this book, she decided that too few people had heard about the bravery of the Grimké sisters. She nominated Sarah and Angelina Grimké for the National Women's Hall of Fame in Seneca Falls, New York. When the sisters were inducted into the hall of fame in the summer of 1998, Stephanie, her husband, and her two grown daughters traveled to Seneca Falls for the ceremony.

A former high school English teacher, McPherson lives in Virginia but also calls California home. She has written many newspaper and magazine stories and several books for children, including *Ordinary Genius: The Story of Albert Einstein* and *Peace and Bread: The Story of Jane Addams,* both published by Carolrhoda Books.

About the Illustrator

Karen Ritz has been practicing drawing since she was a child living in upstate New York. She later moved to Minnesota and earned a degree in children's literature from the University of Minnesota. Since then, she has combined two of her favorite pastimes, reading and drawing, by becoming a children's book illustrator. Ms. Ritz lives in St. Paul with her husband and three children. She has illustrated many children's books, including several for Carolrhoda Books.